CW00657336

who are you following?

guided journal

SADIE ROBERTSON HUFF

THOMAS NELSON
Since 1798

Who Are You Following? Guided Journal

Published in Nashville, Tennessee, by Thomas Nelson. Thomas Nelson is a registered trademark of HarperCollins Christian Publishing, Inc.

Unless otherwise noted, all images courtesy of Sadie Robertson Huff.

Images on pages 93 and 122 sourced from Shutterstock.

Thomas Nelson titles may be purchased in bulk for educational, business, fundraising, or sales promotional use. For information, please email SpecialMarkets@ThomasNelson.com.

Any internet addresses, phone numbers, or company or product information printed in this book are offered as a resource and are not intended in any way to be or to imply an endorsement by Thomas Nelson, nor does Thomas Nelson vouch for the existence, content, or services of these sites, phone numbers, companies, or products beyond the life of this book.

Illustrations by Courtney Leatherwood.

ISBN 978-1-4002-3292-5

Printed in the United States

22 23 24 25 26 JOS 10 9 8 7 6 5 4 3 2 1

contents

introduction

Hey friends! Welcome to our journal. I say *our* journal because it is one that you and I get to share together. I wanted to create a beautiful space for us to reflect on who we are and who we want to be. Because this is a journal, I guess I need to be as open with you as I can be, so why don't I just start off with a bang? I have struggled with anxiety, insecurity, comparison, jealousy, and perfectionism. And although I might have once assumed that saying those things would shock you, I bet it doesn't surprise you at all, does it? Because don't most of us struggle with those things at some point or another?

I will never forget sitting in a meeting at a college with the presidents of every sorority, as girl after girl admitted her struggles with all these things. As I sat and pondered the idea that each of us struggled with such similar challenges, I began to wonder why. Why are we all getting these results at the end of the day? And I wondered, *Does it actually have to be this way?*

After prayer—and some ups and downs myself—I can more clearly see why we may all be in this same toxic pattern. I'll go ahead and answer those questions for you, because I don't want you to go another second without knowing the answers I've found to be true.

Why are we getting these results? I would say it's almost as if we are all following the same cheat sheet that the world handed us for the test of life. But the world got the answers one bubble off. We are all searching for the same things: peace, freedom, joy, contentment, confidence, truth, and love . . . but we are finding anxiety, depression, insecurity, comparison, jealousy, lust, confusion, and more. And it's because of who and what we are following—a cheat sheet that is a bubble off.

"How do you fight for freedom if you do not know that you are a slave?"

I finally reached a point where I said *enough is enough*. I serve a God who says that I can live an abundant life, so why am I drowning? Instead of following an irrelevant cheat sheet, I started studying real truth. And I can gladly tell you that since I finally stopped following every new trend of the world, I started to find the things only God can give me. Because of that, my life has been renewed. I would say that my life is new, but *renew* is a better word because I feel as though I am back to the original person God created me to be. I am not perfect and never will be, but I am free. And so I would like to answer the second question—no, it does *not* have to be this way. There is a God who says, "Seek and you will find," and I want to reassure you that when you start following Him, you'll find Him and so much more.

I recently watched an interview of a person who escaped from North Korea. The interviewer was asking her why the people in her country had not tried to fight for freedom, and she said, "How do you fight for freedom if you do not know that you are a slave?"

In a very different context, and obviously on a vastly different level, I could see how her wisdom applies to many areas. This is why many of us have not looked for an alternative to the things we are struggling with—because we don't even realize there is a struggle! We think, *If everyone is like this, then this must be normal.* I once heard Pastor Sean Smith say, "There is a big difference between the word *normal* and the word *typical.*"

Let's say you go to the doctor feeling sick, and the doctor says, "You have a cold—this is normal." If you are used to being healthy, this sickness is not normal; it may be typical, but it is not normal. In the same way, the things you are walking through may be *typical*, but they are not *normal*. Slowly, subtly, and in line with droves of others, we have allowed the world to shape so many facets of our lives and behaviors without stopping to realize how *not normal* some of them are. In some cases we've shackled ourselves to ideals and influencers and these *very typical* lives we don't actually like. We seek and follow things that drain us instead of fill us.

And we think it's normal . . . but it's not.

A life of freedom is available, but there is only one way to get there. We have to trade in that cheat sheet and start searching for the truth. We have to let Jesus Christ be our guide.

Who you are following is who is influencing you. Who or what you are investing your time in is who is influencing you, and that includes how you spend your time and your money, how you live out your relationships, how you determine what goals you are chasing—or not chasing—and so much more. We're all trying to grow and build meaningful lives, but so often what we're building isn't meaningful. It's broken and not quite enough to satisfy or allow us to feel purposeful.

> We have to trade in that cheat sheet and start searching for the truth.

With so much noise in the secular culture, and how much we immerse ourselves in that culture, it's easy to feel lost. It's easy to search for the way forward, to latch on to someone—anyone— like who you wish you could be or who has a life you wish you had. It's easy to get lost following an idea of someone else's life, and then the next thing you know, you don't recognize the person in your own mirror. Trust me, the times I have followed the trends of the world too closely and changed my hair, makeup, clothes, and whatever else I could to model "the look"—thinking that is what I needed to feel confident—I always came up short.

I may be considered a leader, but I am first a follower.

I look back at those seasons, and I see a girl trying to convince herself that she actually *was* the stranger she was becoming. It's easy to get so busy modeling our lives after these influencers and influences that we waste precious energy. Our main focus gets far away from Jesus. Many times, although we may have a desire to look like Jesus, we end up looking more like the influencers on social media, the celebrities we watch on TV, or even the pastors at our church. Because the truth is, that is who we are really following.

You may be asking, "How can you, Sadie Rob-Huff, with a social media following of millions and big speaking engagements, possibly scrutinize the very social media platforms that have given you an 'audience'?" Fair question. I've had to think about this myself.

First, I am not bashing those platforms. I am grateful for them and believe they are an opportunity for good. But my goal is to make my platform about Jesus, not about me. If you are following me, I will always tell you that I am not leading you to me. That would offer you very little. I don't want you to try to be

FOLLOW
JESUS
ABOVE
ALL

me—I want you to be the unique, whole, and wonderful person Jesus made *you* to be. I won't always get it exactly right, but I want to use my influence to lead you to Jesus. In Him we can find peace, hope, joy, and contentment. In blindly following people, we too often find anxiety, comparison traps, and discontentment. I may be considered a leader, but I am first a follower.

Jesus is the only leader and influencer worth following because He is the essence of all you are searching for. Once you put your energy into following Jesus, and all that this entails—the good, the bad, and especially the challenging—you will feel the freedom to stop looking for all those other things. Worldly platforms and positions, the accumulation of things that aren't bringing you joy, superficial relationships that make you feel empty—those will pale in comparison to what you find in Jesus.

So, my friends, the search is over and you have found what you are looking for, but the journey has just begun. There's no shame here and no judgment. We're all on this journey in some way. Now, let's learn how to redirect our steps and follow Jesus above all.

who is influencing you?

Do you ever find yourself picking up your phone and immediately heading to your Instagram app? I'm raising my hand over here. I can't begin to tell you how many times I've deleted that app from my phone. Sometimes I get in the habit of tapping, deleting, and downloading again. And repeat. I do this because I get tired of how I start to feel when I use social media too much. I get tired of the comparison.

I get tired of the hateful comments. I get tired of feeling like I need to do more, buy more, post more, or look more like something I am not. Have you ever felt this way?

Together we're going to kick some unhealthy habits to the curb. Social media can only be as healthy as we are. And yes, social media *can be healthy*.

This journal is all about discovering who we are following and how we are influenced. We're going to take a personal inventory and become better followers and leaders—both on social media *and* off.

choose who you follow

If you're reading the book and this journal, you're interested in these questions: Who am I following? And why does it matter who we follow?

We have to realize that who we are following is influencing our lives. I believe this is an important part of the process. Before we can be leaders, we have to be followers. In addition, we have to really know and pay attention to *who* we are following and *what* is influencing us. I want you to know that there is an ultimate Influencer who we need to follow on a daily basis.

You can follow trends of the world, or you can follow Jesus.

We all get to choose who we follow, and we get to choose what we allow to lead our lives. I hear people complain that their social media is full of negative stuff, and yes, social media can be negative, but that also depends on who you are following and what you are allowing yourself to see. Life outside of our phones is the same—there are negative influences

and things that will lead us in the wrong direction, just like there are positive influences that will lead us in a good direction. You get to steward who and what you choose to follow. You can follow trends of the world, or you can follow Jesus. I am not saying go unfollow everyone, because there are a lot of great people who genuinely are positive influences. Some make us laugh, some teach us how to do our makeup, some preach or write—so many people are using their giftings that God gave them.

Taking time to assess who we follow will help us know who influences us the most and what we can do about it.

We should all ask ourselves questions before we start following someone: Are they actually leading me where I want to go? Will this person help me be both a better follower and a better leader?

Let's walk you through a "follower checklist." This may sound harsh, but I believe that taking time to assess who we follow will help us know who influences us the most and what we can do about it. Keep in mind that I'm not just talking about famous influencers. There may be friends or colleagues who are leading you down a bad path. That doesn't mean you have to literally unfollow them, but it is good to be aware of who is leading and where they are leading.

follower checklist

1. Who do you follow who builds you up and encourages you? Make a list of those you think are good influences and then write about what those people do that positively affects your life.

— My dad. Being by my side, supporting me in every aspect. He has a strong will power, always learning and seek for knowledges. Love his family with his whole heart. Putting others before himself. Very smart, quick to understand. I wanna learn from him.

— Chloe, very good leader of CV. Make everyone feel included & comfortable around her. Strong believer of God

— Selina, very hard working. Make things work the way she wants in her live, kind to everyone

2. Are you following anyone who brings you down? Who are they and what is it about these people or feeds that bring you down?

Luke

_____

_____

_____

_____

_____

_____

_____

_____

_____

_____

_____

3. Do any of those people you listed in question two also bring you down in real life? How is the experience the same or different when it happens online versus when it happens in person?

_____

_____

_____

_____

_____

_____

_____

_____

_____

_____

_____

_____

4. How often do the people you're following make you feel less than you are? Weekly? Every day? When they post a certain type of content?

_____

_____

_____

_____

_____

_____

_____

_____

_____

_____

_____

_____

5. Do you tend to want more material things or feel more discontent after viewing content from the people you follow?

Sometimes I would wanna buy the clothes that looks good on the influencer.

6. Why do you follow people? What attracts you to follow someone?

_____

_____

_____

_____

_____

_____

_____

_____

_____

_____

_____

_____

7. Are you afraid to unfollow anyone? If so, why?

Yes, some people care so much about followers. They ~~t~~ would take it offensive when I unfollow them, or they thinks that I don't like them so I unfollow. (These are some old friends from high school)

_____

_____

_____

Friend, I know those questions weren't easy to walk through. I hope you felt the freedom to answer openly and honestly. The purpose of this journal is for you to discover who you are following and who you are influenced by—and then to make changes that will impact your life for the better.

As you look at your answers, spend time today and in the coming weeks reflecting on what you wrote. Did any of your answers surprise you? Were you honest with yourself? I pray this exercise brings to light truths about how social media influences your life. And I hope you return to the follower checklist anytime you need another check-in on what you are allowing to influence your life.

fresh social media habits

Anytime I hear the word "habits" I think of eating well and taking care of my body. But there's so much more to our healthy habits than just eating and exercising. Our habits affect us in every area of our lives—physically, mentally, emotionally, and spiritually. As we take inventory of who we follow and how we are influenced, let's look at how much time we spend on social media. I pray this allows us to shift our focus off of who we are following and on to Jesus.

Let's connect the dots and reset our habits so that we can be healthy and fruitful followers.

THERE IS
LIGHT
AND LIFE
IN JESUS.

CURRENT	HEALTHY
How much time do I spend on social media daily? (Check your screen time!)	What's a healthy amount of time to spend on social media daily?
How much time do I spend in the Word?	How much time can I take to spend on my relationship with God (in the Word, worshipping, meeting with a good friend, or watching a sermon online)?
Who do I need to unfollow?	How will I be intentional with those in my sphere of influence (large or small) while on social media?

The way we spend our time often reveals what we care about most. Now that you've looked at how much time you spend on social media, what do you think? I pray that you will be filled with the confidence to step into your healthy social media habits.

the ultimate follow

Our greatest source of life comes from Jesus. In *Who Are You Following?*, I loved sharing about the source of abundant life.

who is influencing you?   15

In John 14:6 Jesus tells us, "I am the way and the truth and the life." And I wholeheartedly believe that if we are following Jesus, we will be full of life. Galatians tells us that the fruit of the Spirit is love, joy, peace, patience, kindness, goodness, faithfulness, gentleness, and self-control. When we follow Jesus, we are bearing fruit in our lives by keeping in step with the Spirit (Galatians 5:25). And we can experience an overflow of God's provision—instead of anxiety, peace; instead of loneliness, love; instead of jealousy, joy.

think about this:

What does it mean for you to follow Jesus today?

meditate on the following verses:

- JOHN 8:12 (ESV): Jesus spoke to them, saying, "I am the light of the world. Whoever follows me will not walk in darkness, but will have the light of life."
- MATTHEW 16:24 (ESV): Then Jesus told his disciples, "If anyone would come after me, let him deny himself and take up his cross and follow me."
- GALATIANS 5:22–26: But the fruit of the Spirit is love, joy, peace, forbearance, kindness, goodness, faithfulness, gentleness and self-control. Against such things there is no law. Those who belong to Christ Jesus have crucified the flesh with its passions and desires. Since we live by the Spirit, let us keep in step with the Spirit. Let us not become conceited, provoking and envying each other.

- DEUTERONOMY 31:8: The LORD himself goes before you and will be with you; he will never leave you nor forsake you. Do not be afraid; do not be discouraged.
- HEBREWS 13:5–6 (ESV): Keep your life free from love of money, and be content with what you have, for he has said, "I will never leave you nor forsake you." So we can confidently say, "The Lord is my helper; I will not fear; what can man do to me?"

ENCOURAGEMENT

You may be struggling like I did, following everything the world throws at us and feeling lost in a sea of stress, insecurity, and uncertainty. The good news is you're just a follow away from a different influence.

prayer

God, thank You for being the ultimate influencer. I pray that You will continue to be the loudest voice in my life. Will Your Spirit guide me and direct my steps to be Your follower?

Help me to be an encouragement to others on social media and in my life. Continue to use me to build others up for the sake of Your good and Your glory. Amen.

what are you seeking?

n John 1:35–41 we find two of Jesus' followers at a critical moment. They finally found the one they had been seeking—Jesus. At their immediate recognition of Him, they dropped all they had and followed Him.

We see in this story how they were able to stop searching and just start *following*, because they first knew what they were looking for. Isn't that how it works—you stop searching when you find what you're looking for? When I met Christian, there was no sense in still looking for someone to marry. The search was over.

If I had to take a guess, I would say that you are probably searching for something right now. Maybe for happiness or purpose? Maybe love or peace? You know, the things in life that we all really desire.

I've searched for the same things in my own life too. This search has led me to look in a lot of places: my relationships, my career, my location. However, I always came up short of finding what my soul was longing for. That is, of course, until I found Jesus. Then the search was over.

The truth is, I found Jesus several times and yet was still searching for those things I mentioned above. It came down to this: when I surrendered my life to Him and followed Him, I found what I was looking for. I realized that you can find Jesus and not follow Him. Finding Christian is not what made him my husband. If we had never followed through with daily phone calls, texts, dates, and long drives to see each other—sometimes just for the day—then we would not have the relationship we do. The following part is the key.

> It came down to this: when I surrendered my life to Him and followed Him, I found what I was looking for.

I am going to bring up social media and our phones a lot. Mainly because that is where we spend a lot of our time—searching aimlessly and following without much thought to what we are allowing ourselves to be influenced by. This influence and direction probably hold more power over your life than you realize. So together we are going to make sure that we have a healthy perspective of what we are viewing daily as we scroll, search, and follow.

My hope for this portion of our time together is that we begin to gain a clearer picture of what we are seeking in our lives. It is easy to get lost online, to waste time wandering, to be lost in the search, and to lose sight of what we ultimately should be seeking. As long as we stay lost in the search, we will come up short of finding what we know will fill our lives.

First, we need to establish what we are seeking so that we can ask ourselves if we are looking in the right places and following the right path to get us there. If I were to lose my keys, I wouldn't go looking in some pond I have never been around—I would look in the car or in the house. I would make sure I was on the path that could lead me to what I was missing.

So let me ask you, What is it that you are *truly* seeking?

Let's take a moment and quiet our hearts and minds and give space for a personal inventory of what we are seeking. Use the page to write down anything that comes to mind. This is a place for you to be open and honest, so don't hold back.

Here are a few questions to ask yourself as you meditate on this:

- What are the areas of my life that I give most of my time to?
- How do I spend the majority of my time online? What am I watching, reading, and scrolling through on my phone?
- What are the deepest desires within my heart?
- When I think about what is *most* important to me, what comes to mind?
- What music, movies, and apps take up the most space in my life? Keep in mind—these can be positive things too!

① - University, lectures, work, Christian group
   Play tennis
② - YouTube shorts, cooking, ~~modeling~~, music, cool videos
③ - Wanna 被 認 同
   - Be a person that God likes.
   - e Have right fruit sprite.
④ - Family, God, friends
   - Exercise, tennis   - Music, piano
⑤ - Christian music, music that I like
   - Anime, TV show (Demon slayer, The office)
   - Youtube, wastapp, candy crush (only in HK)
   - Album, looking at pictures.

Seek
JESUS

This is important to break down because chances are, what you seek you will find—and what you find is what will influence your life.

the power of influence

We all have those people we follow on social media who we think are the coolest humans ever, right? A girl I follow posts the yummiest, healthiest-looking meals for her family. I have personally seen how seeking and following her has influenced my life. I have bought many of the things she puts out with her "swipe up" links. I now have a new blender, her cookbook, and healthier food in the kitchen. Not all social media influence has to be negative! You may follow pastors and ministries online and be influenced in life-changing ways—and that is amazing. But as we know, it can also be easy to go down a negative path if the ones you are seeking and following don't line up with who you are or who you want to be.

Now let's revisit that list above and take it a step further. How are the things that I am seeking having an influence on me? Are they producing godly fruit in my life, like the things we talked about in the last chapter—love, joy, peace, patience, kindness, goodness, faithfulness, gentleness, and self-control (Galatians 5:22–23)?

Now that we are aware of what we are seeking and what is influencing our lives, let's consider what we want to keep seeking and what we need to shift our eyes away from. Go back to the list and circle the things that are worth seeking and that produce godly fruit in your life. Cross out the things that you need to stop following.

WHAT AM I SEEKING?	HOW IS THIS INFLUENCING ME?
Example: *I spend a significant amount of time on YouTube watching workout videos.*	*I find myself obsessing about the perfect body. I can tell watching the videos often produces anxiety.*

I shared how I follow the girl who makes the beautiful and yummy healthy food. That was not a bad thing to be influenced by. However, in the past following her might have looked like me seeing a really skinny and pretty girl on Instagram and wishing I looked like her. I believed that if I could just look like her, then I would be happy. If I could be that skinny and my skin had that glow, then I would be happy with myself. And so I would buy what she told me to buy so I could be more like her and less like me. This is the pattern that can be so damaging and unhealthy, and that's what I want us to change. Following people and being influenced in ways that drain us will never fulfill us or give us the confidence we are looking for.

What are you really looking for? Are you finding it? What are you getting instead? And where else could you be spending your time?

meditate on the following verses:

- PSALM 63:1: You, God, are my God, earnestly I seek you; I thirst for you, my whole being longs for you, in a dry and parched land where there is no water.
- PROVERBS 4:24–27: Keep your mouth free of perversity; keep corrupt talk far from your lips. Let your eyes look straight ahead; fix your gaze directly before you. Give careful thought to the paths for your feet and be steadfast in all your ways. Do not turn to the right or the left; keep your foot from evil.
- PSALM 9:10: Those who know your name trust in you, for you, LORD, have never forsaken those who seek you.
- PSALM 119:2: Blessed are those who keep his statutes and seek him with all their heart.
- LUKE 11:9–10 (ESV): And I tell you, ask, and it will be given to you; seek, and you will find; knock, and it will be opened to you. For everyone who asks receives, and the one who seeks finds, and to the one who knocks it will be opened.
- JEREMIAH 29:13 (NASB): You will seek Me and find Me when you search for Me with all your heart.

74

Once we
find Jayda, he
our parents. We k
from our family. And w

Remember, you'll never reach an amount of likes or followers that will fulfill you. You can never swipe up on enough links to become someone you are not. If who you are right now is not enough for you, then it will never become enough for the add-ons the world can offer. Stop the scrolling and searching and allow God to remind you of who He created. Don't get lost in the search.

ENCOURAGEMENT
You have the power to stop following whatever might be leading you down a bad path. Now is the time to shift your eyes!

prayer

God, I want to seek You first. I confess that I often find my heart seeking other things that are not of You and do not draw me closer to You. Empower me, by Your Spirit, to seek after You with all my heart. I know that You are the only thing that will ever truly satisfy me. I am running after You with my whole heart.

from liked
to loved

There's a big difference between being liked and being loved. The words *like* and *love* are so similar, yet the realities of each are vastly different. It can be easy in our world to use these words interchangeably, but understanding the distinction between them is life-changing.

The definition of *being liked* includes being agreeable, enjoyable, and able to bring satisfaction. The social media definition of *liked* includes winning someone's approval. We post our best angles, highlight our brightest days, and edit our true feelings and struggles to make ourselves seem more likable.

On the flipside, to be *loved* is to be truly known. To be known in our messy states, our unpolished and imperfect selves, but still understood inside and out—and still deeply treasured and held. To be loved requires vulnerability, authenticity, and the freedom of allowing ourselves to be truly known—while being liked requires very little commitment and authenticity.

Let's break down these two words so we are clear on what they really mean:

TRUE "LIKE"	TRUE "LOVE"
To be agreeable	Casts out all fear
To be seen	Allows you to be known, not just seen
To be enjoyable	Cares about you even when you are hurting
To bring satisfaction	Doesn't need you to do anything to feel more worthy
To win approval	Knows that you were created to be enough

perfection is exhausting

Do you ever find yourself wanting to be liked or accepted? I can think of so many times that I have. In those cases I was trying to look perfect, act perfect, and say everything perfectly—it was absolutely exhausting to chase perfection. If you have experienced that same situation of trying to be liked, journal about your memories.

Many times I acted like I know what the person is talking about. So that I might look smart or not asking a question that everyone know the answer, (Might look dumb)

Staying in the UK for so many years that people expect me to be like locals. The truths is that, I'm not. seqzcially in boarding school, I didn't really see the world outside. And I couldn't spreak English.

I've found that there is often more pressure in being *liked* than *loved*. I often share the story about when Christian and I were dating. Deep in the *like* stage (you know, before we said the big "I love you" phrase), I was trying to present myself in the best possible light—the perfect tan, fresh nails, and my outfit always on point. It was a lot of pressure to keep up. Not pressure that Christian was putting on me—but pressure that kept me working to keep up with the standard of being *liked*.

Fast-forward to just after we had finished one of our most honest and vulnerable talks where we both shared difficult things about our pasts—it was then that we finally told each other "I

LIVE
LOVED

love you." We were not trying to win approval. It was not pretty. It was not enjoyable. It was not *like* . . . it was *love*.

This was a moment we shared together that was hard and real—and ended with us feeling truly known and loved by each other.

1. Have you ever considered bending who you are or making yourself more likable in a relationship? This could be a new dating relationship, hanging around a new group of friends, or another scenario.

— Yes, Pretended that I like something, same as the other person. To win approval,
— Priortis the other person's choice before mine. Putting other first.

2. If so, how did that make you feel? Was it easy to keep
up? Imagine how the relationship or friendship might look
different if operated out of love instead of like.

- It felt wrong to lie. Hard to keep up.
Eventually we do not have out as much.
- It feels good that other person is satisfy.
Allows me to try new things.
Liking or experiencing others hobby or
restrearent.

We're going to take this one step further to help identify the practical differences between being liked and being loved, and what it means to live that out.

I'M STRIVING TO BE LIKED WHEN I . . .	I KNOW I AM LOVED WHEN I . . .
Try to say everything perfectly.	Can speak freely from my heart.
Do everything that the other person wants.	Do things that we like together,

The Like button is familiar to many. It feels good to be seen and validated. So good in fact, that we keep going back to it over and over again. Looking at the table above, what are ways you find yourself striving to be liked instead of knowing that you are loved? What are the pitfalls keeping you living in the *like* instead of *love*?

I still fight the temptation to strive for likes, whether on social media or in my life. When I feel the need to "perform" instead of being myself, I take a step back and hit the reset button. Sometimes that looks like going a few days without wearing makeup. Sometimes that looks like allowing myself to speak before I have the perfect thing to say. Other times, it looks like posting the picture just because *I like the picture* and not because others will.

Loving ourselves and being comfortable with who God created us to be can save us from many pitfalls both on and off the Internet. I was dating a guy when I first started to get some traction with my speaking engagements and began speaking to larger and larger crowds. He came to one of the events where I was speaking in front of about ten thousand people, and there was an autograph and picture-signing line afterward. It was pretty eye-opening for him to see that side of me when we had just been casually dating.

Even when you're not likable, you're loved.

After that night, he started being extremely rude and talked down to me for the next few days, and I didn't know why. I confronted him about the way he was treating me, and he said something along the lines of: "Just so you know, I'm not going to be one of your little fans who holds you up on a pedestal and claps for you everywhere you go." I was stunned. With tears welling up in my eyes, I got out of his car and said, "I can't be in this relationship anymore." After seeing all these people cheer for me and applaud for me, he was basically trying to humble me, but it wasn't out of love. And since I was struggling to love myself, I really didn't need to be humbled in that way.

He didn't care to understand what I was going through, what I'd been through, or how I really felt. The truth is, I was struggling with the pressure of so many people watching me, and he failed to really know my heart. He treated me terribly based on what he saw and assumed.

Just because people see you doesn't mean they know what you're going through. And the same goes for how you view and interact with others. The guy I dated thought that I was successful and that everything was easy for me. But he didn't know what was in my heart or that I was struggling. We don't need to be influenced by people who make us feel small, and we don't have to stay in situations that make us feel uncomfortable or in relationships that are toxic. The more comfortable we can get with not always being *liked* and the more secure we are in being truly *loved*, the less likely we are to let negative influences drag us down.

In 1 John, we are reminded that "perfect love casts out fear" (4:18 ESV). True love allows us to be fully known by God—in all our filth, in our pasts, in the little things we don't want others to see—yet still wholly loved. God's love is never-ending. Even when you're not likable, you're loved. Instead of the insecurity from the likes or lack thereof, this perfect love brings complete security because it doesn't change based on your actions or transgressions.

think about this:

Who in your life knows you well and still offers unconditional love? Who, in turn, do you show unconditional love to? Here are a few more things to ponder about yourself and your relationships:

- Do you have more pictures with people than actual memories with them?
- Do you spend more time looking at your phone than you do talking to the people with you?
- Do you know more about people's lives than the highlight reel they put on social media?
- Do you check in on your friends in real life as much as you slide up on people's stories?
- Are you the same person you portray on social media?

- PSALM 139:1: You have searched me, LORD, and you know me.
- ROMANS 8:38–39 (KJV): For I am convinced that neither death, nor life, nor angels, nor principalities, nor things present, nor things to come, nor powers, nor height, nor depth, nor any other created thing will be able to separate us from the love of God that is in Christ Jesus our Lord.
- 1 JOHN 4:18–19 (NASB): There is no fear in love; but perfect love drives out fear, because fear involves punishment, and the one who fears is not perfected in love. We love, because He first loved us.

ENCOURAGEMENT

God sees you right where you are and loves you before you ever do a thing. You do not have to strive for His love. It is freely given.

prayer

Lord, thank You for being the ultimate definition of love. I pray that I would no longer seek to be liked but rest in knowing that I am loved. Thank You for choosing us, for loving us, and for calling us heirs as Your children.

who are you comparing yourself to?

Comparison is never pretty, yet we continue to regularly fall into its trap. In a recent poll that I posted on my Instagram story, I learned that 91 percent of girls compare their images to their friends'. I would say that I'm shocked, but sadly this is not surprising. Pretty much everyone I talk to says they struggle with comparison! Funny enough, this poll happened inside of Instagram, the very platform that encourages this type of behavior.

So, who do you compare yourself to?

Friends, sisters, family, celebrities, moms—I'm sure the list goes on of those you look at, size up, and so much more. What if I told you there was a way out? A way to stop falling into the comparison trap?

Romans 12:2 (esv) says, "Do not be conformed to this world, but be transformed by the renewal of your mind, that by testing you may discern what is the will of God, what is good and acceptable and perfect." This is my go-to verse when I get complacent with things like comparison. It's one of those things that can be easy to just hold on to because *everyone struggles with it, right?* The Word of God does not say, "If everyone struggles then you get a pass." The Word says not to be conformed to the pattern of this world. It then says to transform your mind! I want to transform my mind to stop comparing myself to my sisters around the world and to celebrate them instead.

> I want to transform my mind to stop comparing myself to my sisters around the world and to celebrate them instead.

why can't i be just like her?

Before we dive deeper, I want to be upfront about something. You can't be just like her. *Period.*

But *why?* Why can I not have her body? Why can I not have her life? Why?! Simply put, because you're not her. God did not make you just like her, because He had something else in mind for you. And while we're on the subject—no one can be just like you!

You may have been telling yourself the same lie many girls

tell themselves. You may think that you will be confident when you get what she has, look the way she does, and succeed so people notice you like they notice her. But the confidence won't come from looking like her or getting the likes she has. The kind of confidence that you are looking for will not be found in achieving something someone else has.

You are called to live in the fullness of you.

Confidence will come when you have security in who you are! You could live your whole life trying to be like *her*, but you'll always be a lesser version of her. Not because you are less than, but simply because you cannot live in the fullness of someone else—you are called to live in the fullness of *you*.

Spend a few minutes journaling your thoughts to the questions below:

1. Is there an area of your life where you're trying to be like someone else? Write out every area that comes to mind.

I would put on british accent in
class. So I don't stand out when
I speak. My face already stand out
(the only asian) At the same time I
like I'm the only few asian in the
crew. Feels like I blend in with others,

Wear ~~that~~ similar clothes as the girls who I think looks good.

2. What would it be like if you committed to being who God made you to be? What behaviors need to change to help you get there?

I don't have a clear vision of what God made me to be.

- Putting God as my focus, not guys around me

- Dress confidable, not those that attract others.

- Covering more. Not shaving.

- ~~X lust~~ X lust

celebrate your sisters

3. Stop for a minute and imagine being at peace with who God made you to be. Close your eyes and take a deep breath. Imagine all the comparison traps and need for approval falling away. Write about how that makes you feel.

_____

_____

_____

_____

_____

_____

_____

_____

_____

_____

_____

_____

_____

_____

wonderfully made

Psalm 139:13–16 (ᴇsv) says, "For you formed my inward parts; you knitted me together in my mother's womb. I praise you, for I am fearfully and wonderfully made. Wonderful are your works; my soul knows it very well. My frame was not hidden from you, when I was being made in secret, intricately woven in the depths of the earth. Your eyes saw my unformed substance."

I love that David wrote this. His soul knew full well that he was fearfully and wonderfully made. You might say it was easy for him—he was a king, a hero, a musician, and he killed lions and bears with his own hands. But if you remember the story, that same David was the last pick of all his brothers.

And if I know anything about insecurity, it's that it doesn't matter how far life takes you or what you achieve. You can still hold on to things people said about you in the past and compare yourself to others. I once had the opportunity to model at New York Fashion Week, and *even then* I was insecure because I still saw myself for what people had said about me in the past. It was so easy to compare myself to every girl walking beside me instead of being content in my own skin.

I find it so sad that the Enemy distorts the view of beauty we once had as little girls.

When we are little kids, it seems like we are all confident. We don't care what we look like, and if we do, it's usually because we think we look awesome. I saw two of my little cousins staring at themselves in a mirror recently, and I was struck by the confidence they had. I want to look in a mirror and see how they see! I thought to myself, *Why don't I?* I'm sure I used to. The hard truth is that at some point I began believing that the Original Artist was not as talented as the temporary, vaporlike trends of the world. I thought His creation wasn't as good as the standard of beauty that was presented to me.

I find it so sad that the Enemy distorts the view of beauty we once had as little girls. My baby girl is absolutely beautiful in my eyes, and I don't compare her to a single thing—just like I wasn't compared to a single thing in my mom's eyes or God's eyes. But at some point I started to look around and think of myself as less than wonderfully made.

1. How hard is it to believe Psalm 139 about ourselves? Let's be real. Take a few moments and journal what you believe about what God's Word says in Psalm 139. (See the full passage at the end of this chapter.)

_____

_____

_____

_____

_____

_____

_____

_____

2. Have you been feeling "less than"?

_____

_____

_____

_____

_____

_____

_____

_____

_____

3. Can you trace that feeling back to a lie you've believed or even a lie spoken over you?

_____

_____

_____

_____

_____

_____

_____

_____

_____

_____

If there were any words spoken over you that bring insecurity, we're going to pause and pray: *God, I confess that it's hard for me to believe that I am fearfully and wonderfully made. Give me new eyes to see me through Yours. Help me to overcome feelings of comparison and insecurity. Thank You for creating me and loving me just as I am.*

insecurity births insecurity

We've talked about a few unhealthy rhythms of social media and our resulting thoughts. Listen, if you don't get ahold of the insecurity and comparison and competition, it won't just go away. You'll continue to reproduce insecurity, and you'll begin to spread insecurity throughout your group of friends. Like a wildfire, catching tree by tree with a wild flame, we see our own insecurities breed criticism and, instead of lifting up other women, we perpetuate this miserable cycle.

But when you stop feeding insecurity and breeding criticism and instead start praising God, everything changes. You breathe

confidence. You're free to celebrate people for who they are and the things God is doing in their lives. Celebrating others doesn't take away from what you're doing—if it's all for the kingdom, what others do should only add to it. It's important to not only ask yourself if you're taking the place of God but also make sure you're living your life for God and not yourself. This is when your life will be powerful.

Today's the day we lay down the comparison game and competition we have with God and we say, "God, You are good. Therefore—I know because You said it—I am good. And that is not only enough, it is powerful."

Spend a few minutes journaling your thoughts to the questions below:

1. Is there an area of your life in which you're trying to be God?

_____

_____

_____

_____

_____

_____

_____

2. Can you recognize some patterns in your life, with social media, that are affecting the way you view your body?

_____

_____

_____

_____

_____

_____

_____

_____

_____

_____

_____

_____

our thoughts

Our thoughts have the potential to consume us. Who we follow matters because we have a lot of content coming at us from social media. This is the part where we set the record straight . . . no more comparison! Let's align our thoughts with what the Word says about us.

And it's important for us to continue to seek the Word. Reading it will fill your mind, your thoughts, and your soul. This process is not just about stripping away the negative—it's also about filling ourselves and our minds with the good, and the greatest good is God's Word.

ALIGNING GOD'S WORD	ACTION
Do you believe that God formed you? Do you believe that He knit you together?	Name five qualities about *you* that you love. It's not self-centered—we're giving God all the praise!

Do the words that you speak over yourself align with the belief that you're wonderfully made?

What negative things do you say or think about yourself? Replace those with positive things.

Do your daily actions align with the belief that you are wonderfully made?

What are three things you could do today to treat your mind and body with love and care? Name them and do them!

I have personally found it helpful to thank God for the function of my body parts instead of their appearance. Instead of saying, "I wish I had skinnier or more fit legs," I say, "Thank You that my legs are able to walk and get me where I am going." "Thank You that my arms can carry things and my hands can write and type." "Thank You that my stomach was able to carry a baby inside of it." Exchanging complaint for gratitude gives us such an appreciation for the body that we have and for God who created it.

> Our words and thoughts reveal what we believe about ourselves and about God.

I trust that your answers are honest and true to where you are in this moment. Our words and thoughts reveal what we believe about ourselves and about God. This journal time is designed for you to step away and really consider the condition of your heart and mind. Be encouraged, and return to these questions regularly. Soak in His Word and let His truth wash over any insecurity.

If you let God's Word be what makes you feel seen and known and loved, then you won't have to struggle with comparison.

think about this:

Are you looking around at others wishing you had what they had? Where is that temptation coming from?

Psalm 139

You have searched me, Lord,
    and you know me.
You know when I sit and when I rise;
    you perceive my thoughts from afar.
You discern my going out and my lying down;
    you are familiar with all my ways.
Before a word is on my tongue
    you, Lord, know it completely.
You hem me in behind and before,
    and you lay your hand upon me.
Such knowledge is too wonderful for me,
    too lofty for me to attain.
Where can I go from your Spirit?
    Where can I flee from your presence?
If I go up to the heavens, you are there;
    if I make my bed in the depths, you are
        there.
If I rise on the wings of the dawn,
    if I settle on the far side of the sea,
even there your hand will guide me,
    your right hand will hold me fast.
If I say, "Surely the darkness will hide me
    and the light become night around me,"
even the darkness will not be dark to you;
    the night will shine like the day,
    for darkness is as light to you.

For you created my inmost being;
you knit me together in my
mother's womb.
I praise you because I am fearfully and
wonderfully made;
your works are wonderful,
I know that full well.
My frame was not hidden from you
when I was made in the secret place,
when I was woven together in the depths
of the earth.
Your eyes saw my unformed body;
all the days ordained for me were written
in your book
before one of them came to be.
How precious to me are your thoughts, God!
How vast is the sum of them!
Were I to count them,
they would outnumber the grains
of sand—
when I awake, I am still with you.
If only you, God, would slay the wicked!
Away from me, you who are
bloodthirsty!
They speak of you with evil intent;
your adversaries misuse your name.
Do I not hate those who hate you, LORD,
and abhor those who are in rebellion
against you?
I have nothing but hatred for them;
I count them my enemies.

Search me, God, and know my heart;
    test me and know my anxious thoughts.
See if there is any offensive way in me,
    and lead me in the way everlasting.

ENCOURAGEMENT

You are you for a reason, and the sooner you come to that revelation, the sooner you will live a life of freedom.

Prayer

God, I thank You that You made me fearfully and wonderfully in Your image. I acknowledge that You made me original and unique. I pray that Your Spirit would help me to no longer compare myself to those around me but rather celebrate them for who they are.

why do you want to be famous?

Fame is a funny thing. It makes humans who are no different from any other humans seem like gods. It causes people to scream, cry, faint, and react in quite strange ways over someone they don't even know. I get it, though. I have been a huge fan of *Family Feud* for as long as I can remember. As soon as I turn the TV on, I see if there is an episode of *Family Feud* playing. Back in 2015, my family got the opportunity to go on the show, and when Steve Harvey walked out, I am embarrassed to say that I cried. *Cried!* When he walked over to introduce himself, I was a snotty, tear-filled dweeb. Why does fame do this to us?

fame by the numbers

- A study found that "many 18–25-year-olds said that their desire for fame was the first or second most important life goal."[1] Now, being a YouTube star, Instagram influencer, or TikTok famous is more sought-after than becoming a doctor or a lawyer.
- One out of nine millennials would rather be famous than get married. One in ten would rather be famous than get a college degree. A few of the study's participants would even disown their own family if it meant they would become famous.[2]
- The more you use social media, the more important fame becomes to you, according to a recent UCLA study.[3]

There are so many reasons why people seek fame or outward, worldly success. First, fame looks pretty fun, doesn't it? When we think of fame we think of lights, camera, action! We think of private jets and crazy trips, sold-out shows, nice clothes, and beautiful couples. It looks like an easy life. Although that's what we see, I think we all know that while fame may look like an abundant life, those enjoying it often admit that fame does not live up to its image. The irony is that people want to be famous to feel accepted, yet famous people often express feeling extremely lonely.

The *New York Times* asked one twenty-six-year-old woman why she believes fame is such a driving force for people her age. She answered, "To be noticed, to be wanted, to be loved, to walk into a place and have others care about what you're doing, even what you had for lunch that day: that's what people want, in my opinion."[4]

I would agree with her, wouldn't you? We all want those things, and those desires in and of themselves are not bad. However, if we expect to meet them through fame, success, or attention, then we will never be satisfied.

> The irony is that people want to be famous to feel accepted, yet famous people often express feeling extremely lonely.

I also want to point out that we don't just search for our desires in fame. We search in college degrees, job security, social status, and even marriage and family. These things can give us a sense of being noticed, wanted, loved, and cared about (at times), but even they cannot totally satisfy our souls. Why? Because they all can fade and fail us.

There is one God, and there is one way that we're going to find the eternal contentment, validation, and joy that we seek— through Him and no one else.

"all you have is all you need"

Pastor Mike Todd says this quote often, and it is so true: "All you have is all you need."[5] I want you to recognize this today so that you can begin to live your life right where you are. Let's make some declarations together.

- I do not have to be more successful, popular, or famous to know that I am accepted. I am accepted by the God who created me as I am.
- I do not have to be in a different location to fulfill my purpose in life. I can make an impact right where I am for the kingdom of God.
- I do not need to gain anything else to know that I have worth. I know I have worth because God chose to create me.

I once saw a girl on a talent show who had cancer. She was given only a 2 percent chance at survival. She mentioned that you cannot wait until life is not hard anymore to choose to be happy.[6] For a while she thought that she would wait until her cancer was gone and then she would go do the things she wanted to do, but then she had the epiphany that her life is now. I want you to hear that same message. Your life is now. It is not waiting for you to reach a level of success to begin. It is now.

I want to point out that fame is not a bad thing. Fame is simply being known. I am famous to some degree, and honestly, so are you. Fame in the church world gets a bad rap because when people become famous, they do not tend to be following Jesus. Those who become famous also do not appear to be very humble. But that is not fame's fault—that is simply people's decisions on how to treat the fame they have. Nothing I mentioned—fame, success, degrees, and so on—are bad things to want and to accomplish. Those are all amazing, but anytime we put something in the place of God we will come up empty-handed.

Let's take a few minutes to think through the things we want most and why we want them.

explore your

PASSIONS

find your

PURPOSE

1. What are you seeking most right now? Think about what you spend your time on, what you daydream about, what you really wish you had.

_____

_____

_____

_____

_____

_____

_____

_____

_____

_____

_____

2. As I mentioned, many things people may be seeking—
   including fame—are not necessarily bad. But they can
   become destructive if we seek them before God or put
   them above all other things in our lives. How are you doing
   in this area? Do your priorities seem healthy and in order?

_____

_____

_____

_____

_____

_____

_____

_____

_____

_____

_____

_____

3. Is there anything you are pursuing right now because of pressure from others rather than personal passion?

_____

_____

_____

_____

_____

_____

_____

_____

_____

_____

_____

purpose and passion

Our calling is not to seek fame but to seek our purpose within God's kingdom. When we do this, we may accidentally find fame. Or we may not. But it won't matter, because we will be living our purpose. One of the questions I get asked most often is, "How do I find my purpose?" Here's a hint: it's already in your heart. God doesn't leave you hanging without purpose. You don't have to wait for your purpose to arrive. Don't search the world around you for the clues; look inside. It's a matter of tuning out the noise and pressures of the world and tuning in to His message. As Christians, our purpose is to love God and love others, and I think our callings are more specific insight as to how we as individuals are going to do that. So what are you passionate about? What do you think God has put in your heart to live out His purpose?

> Don't search the world around you for the clues; look inside.

passion list

You may want to sit down and fill out this list in one sitting, or you may want to come back to it over a period of time, but I'd encourage you to begin listing things that you are sincerely passionate about. Not because it's something trendy or something that gets you a lot of likes but because you really love it.

1. _____

2. _____

3. _____

4. _____

5. _____

6. _____

7. _____

8. _____

9. _____

10. _____

11. _____

12. _____

13. _____

14. _____

15. _____

16. _____

His Glory

In this table I want you to write out things that you are known for and how you can use those things for the glory of God.

WHAT I AM KNOWN FOR	HOW CAN I USE THIS FOR GOD'S GLORY?
Example: People know me as the funny girl in my sorority.	*Example: I could use my humor to make girls feel comfortable. This might give me an opportunity to have meaningful conversations that could lead my friends to know Christ.*

There have been times in my life that I did not feel as though I had a lot to offer. In those moments it's easy to wonder, *God, am I enough for You to use?* It's important to remember that this same God is also the God who created you to be exactly who you are. He is the God who calls you His beloved, accepts you, sees you, and wants you.

think about this:

God can use you right where you are.

meditate on these verses:

- MATTHEW 5:14–16 (ESV): You are the light of the world. A city set on a hill cannot be hidden. Nor do people light a lamp and put it under a basket, but on a stand, and it gives light to all in the house. In the same way, let your light shine before others, so that they may see your good works and give glory to your Father who is in heaven.
- GALATIANS 2:20 (ESV): I have been crucified with Christ. It is no longer I who live, but Christ who lives in me. And the life I now live in the flesh I live by faith in the Son of God, who loved me and gave himself for me.
- 1 JOHN 4:12 (ESV): No one has ever seen God; if we love one another, God abides in us and his love is perfected in us.
- EPHESIANS 2:10 (ESV): For we are his workmanship, created in Christ Jesus for good works, which God prepared beforehand, that we should walk in them.

- PHILIPPIANS 1:6 (ESV): And I am sure of this, that he who began a good work in you will bring it to completion at the day of Jesus Christ.

ENCOURAGEMENT
Look down at yourself and realize that you have all you need to rock the world. You have the Spirit of the living God inside you.

prayer
———

God, thank You for seeing me, loving me, and accepting me as I am. I acknowledge that I do not need fame, money, success, or anything other than what I already have to be enough for You to use for Your glory. Help me, God, to use any bit of success that I do have for Your renown. More of You and less of me, Jesus. Keep me humble as You open any doors that come my way.

06

what are you sharing and why?

When Christian and I were close to getting engaged, we thought it would be really fun to go ring shopping together. However, I did not want to actually pick out my ring, because I wanted it to be a surprise. Secretly, Christian already had my ring when we went shopping.

When we got to the jewelry store, the guy helping us started to ask which rings I liked. I proceeded to just make up which ones I liked, but I truly was not paying attention. I was having fun acting like I was really ring shopping. I even ended up "picking a ring."

Well, when we left, the fun and games were over. I could tell Christian had not had as much fun as I did. He looked super confused. He was also feeling defeated because he thought he'd known what I liked, but apparently the ring I picked was completely different from what he had bought.

"I did not think that ring was something you would have liked," he said. "And I have been looking at a ring that is totally different." In actuality he was not just looking at a ring—he had bought a ring totally different from the one I picked out when I was acting. *Oops.* I felt bad. When I reminded him I was just acting, he said, "Well, you even fooled me!"

when pretending isn't fun

Now we laugh about that story and my impressive acting skills, but at the time it wasn't funny to Christian. He was confused, and I can't blame him for that. He thought he knew what I liked, and here I was showing him something completely different and acting really giddy about it. The truth is, people get confused when we pretend to be someone we are not, and to be completely honest, it ends up confusing *us* more. Especially when we pretend we like things we don't care for and we act in ways that don't represent how we really feel. Pretending seems like a fun option in life, but it never leads us to what we truly want.

When it comes to social media, it's easy to pretend that we are happy and doing great. We share our best photos, coolest trips, and most exciting moments. Once, I was in a relationship that—by social media's standards—looked great. We were what you would call #goals. During that time, I would pretend that I was confident in *who* I was, and that I was happy with *where* I was. I thought by publicly pretending and showing people this image of what I wished to be, it would feel real.

I tried to fool myself.

But the truth others saw on social media wasn't always the truth about my relationship. I can't blame people for commenting on things like our couple's name and couple goals, or wishing they could be like us—I can blame only myself. At that time the sad thing was that my public life seemed much healthier than my private life.

> When it comes to social media, it's easy to pretend that we are happy and doing great.

Publicly I was thriving. I was getting so many likes, comments, and follows because of this cute relationship, but privately I was drowning in my own insecurity. All that pretending publicly didn't make for much fun privately, where I was crying in the shower, confused about who I was and what I really wanted. Take some time to ask yourself these questions:

1. Who am I?

_____

_____

_____

_____

_____

STREAMS
OF LIVING

WATER

_____

_____

_____

_____

_____

2. Am I pretending to be someone I'm not?

_____

_____

_____

_____

_____

_____

_____

_____

3. Who am I pretending to be?

_____

_____

_____

_____

_____

_____

_____

_____

_____

_____

_____

_____

_____

_____

4. Why do I feel the need to pretend?

_____

_____

_____

_____

_____

_____

_____

_____

_____

Think about your answers to the questions above. Sometimes who we really are does not seem as cool or put together as the person people know us to be, so we hesitate to admit the truth. Speaking from personal experience, the real version of you is the greatest version of you, regardless of how uncool or not-put-together it seems. Your private life might not sound as exciting as your public life, but without a healthy private life you will never have a sustaining public life. The real version of you is who God can use to bring Him glory! The real version of you is who will have a real testimony! One that can change lives!

I am guilty of getting on health kicks and jumping on the latest health trends. I love acai bowls and green juices. I love a good kale salad with salmon. And I genuinely like the way I feel when I choose a healthy option. However, I have to admit that there have been times I thought I was being healthy but was actually way off.

Like when I got on a Smoothie King kick. I would go by Smoothie King just about every day for my afternoon snack. A few weeks into this ritual I started noticing myself gaining weight. I couldn't imagine how that could be when I was being "so healthy." Well, friends, turns out that just because it's a smoothie doesn't mean it's healthy. My peanut-power-plus-added-chocolate smoothie was worse than drinking a milkshake every day!

> Just because it looks good doesn't mean it's good.

And yes, you can laugh at me, but you have probably done the same thing! That trail mix we love that we call *healthy* because it has nuts in it, but we all know it's the chocolate chips and M&M's that keep us coming back. Or the birthday cake–flavored protein bar that has frosting and sprinkles that we're calling lunch. Just because something sounds healthy doesn't mean it has the nutrients to sustain like truly healthy food does.

We often try to sustain our inner and spiritual lives with things that aren't actually sufficient. It could be posting a picture of yourself looking all happy and dressed up, but only because you need someone to tell you that you look good. Or going to a Bible study just to say you were there. Maybe it's going to church just to check it off the list. But just because it looks good doesn't mean it is good.

Christian and I love Psalm 1:2–3. In fact, these are our marriage verses. I want you to read it in The Passion Translation.

> His passion is to remain true to the Word of "I AM," meditating day and night on the true revelation of light. He will be standing firm like a flourishing tree planted by God's design, deeply rooted by the brooks of bliss, bearing fruit in every season of life. He is never dry, never fainting, ever blessed, ever prosperous.

To be truly prosperous we must meditate on the Word of God—not the comments of the world.

To Christian and me, the visual of a tree planted by a stream of living water shows the necessity of living by the Word of God, remaining steadfast in our faith, and seeking life from the Lord—and no other sources. When you're rooted strongly in the ground, adversity and hardships cannot topple you. You're able to deal with what comes your way. On the other hand, if you're a small flower or weed living on the daily watering of social media comments, views, likes, and retweets, your shallow roots can easily be pushed and pulled with the wind.

We need more people in the world who are not just pretending to be healthy, but who actually *are* healthy. All the pretending is not going to offer us any help or any health. You will end up like me after weeks of Smoothie King, thinking you have it all figured out but making the problems you face worse. The good news is that you can be healthy in every season if you stand on the promises of God's Word and make your relationship with Him your first priority.

WATER FOR A FLOWER	WATER FOR A TREE
Example: I am trying to feel beautiful through the compliments I get in a day.	*Example: I know I am beautiful because the Word of God says I am fearfully and wonderfully made.*

By rooting yourself in God's Word daily, you can become the healthiest version of yourself. No diet plan can promise you that!

meditate on the following verses:

- PSALM 22:22 (GNT): I will tell my people what you have done; I will praise you in their assembly.

- GALATIANS 1:10 (GW): Am I saying this now to win the approval of people or God? Am I trying to please people? If I were still trying to please people, I would not be Christ's servant.
- ROMANS 8:5–6 (ESV): For those who live according to the flesh set their minds on the things of the flesh, but those who live according to the Spirit set their minds on the things of the Spirit. For to set the mind on the flesh is death, but to set the mind on the Spirit is life and peace.
- PROVERBS 12:22: The LORD detests lying lips, but he delights in people who are trustworthy.
- HEBREWS 13:18: Pray for us. We are sure that we have a clear conscience and desire to live honorably in every way.

ENCOURAGEMENT

Don't fool yourself into believing things are good for you when you know they are not. Seek the things today that truly benefit your today and your tomorrow.

prayer
—

God, I desire to have a healthy private life. Uproot the weeds in my life that I continue to water by the daily showers of the world. I want to be by Your stream of living water. May the health of my private life be the sustainer of my public life. May all that I do bring Your name glory and not my own.

are you following cancel culture?

A number of years ago, when I was still in high school, I was out to eat with my great-grandma. She is one of the most special people to me, and I treasure every moment we have together. In the middle of our lunch a group of people approached me to take a picture. I should mention that on this particular day something had just happened that made me sad, so it was not a great time for a group of people to walk into this conversation.

They asked me for a picture, and I said yes, but I asked if instead of taking individual pictures with everyone if we could take a group shot. They got upset and said they would prefer individual photos. I went on to take the pictures, but apparently I looked annoyed about taking all the pictures separately. Later that day, I saw on my social media that this group of people made some horrible comments telling everyone that I am not who I say I am, not to ever listen to another message of mine, buy another book, or even follow me on social media. I was shocked. I messaged them and apologized for the way that they felt, and I even tried to give them more context to help them understand the moment they stepped into. However, they continued to speak negatively about me.

It was crazy how fast I got canceled by a group of people.

It was crazy how fast I got canceled by a group of people who happened to approach me on a hard day when I was dealing with something privately at lunch with my great-grandma.

For many people, cancel culture seems to be a new concept. Out of nowhere everyone is getting canceled for everything. From my perspective cancel culture isn't new, but we recently put language to it. Sometimes people get canceled because they do something wrong, sometimes they say something wrong, and other times they just have a different opinion than the popular one and that gets them canceled. It makes me sad because it can be so unfair. But in these moments when the world can be so hateful and act as if we have no second chance, I'm thankful for a gospel that says we do.

YOUR
STORY
IS NOT
OVER

The message of the gospel is one of hope and a future, despite the mistakes we have made. The message of Jesus cancels out cancel culture. However, I don't think people always realize that Jesus was misunderstood and highly criticized by many in His lifetime. You might not expect the Son of God to feel such turmoil and struggle, but He did. Just like we all have, and then some. Throughout the Gospels, people were constantly trying to cancel Jesus because He would do and say things the religious leaders of the day deemed politically and religiously incorrect. Luke 11:54 tells it plainly: they were "waiting to catch him in something he might say." In fact, Jesus was the most canceled person in the Bible and in history.

when we cancel jesus

It may have come as a shock to you that Jesus was canceled in His day; not only was He canceled in His day but He gets canceled in ours as well. People are still finding ways to accuse Him and misunderstand Him. We need to check our own hearts as well because we could hop on that cancel-culture train sooner than later if we don't know the truth about who Jesus is for ourselves.

> When we unfollow certain parts of God's character, we miss out on the fullness of who God is.

One of the world's false perspectives of Jesus could cause trouble in our own relationship with Him. I find that sometimes it can be easy to trust only in *some* of the attributes of God and then unfollow other attributes because they might be hard for us to believe or understand. Take a look at this list and meditate on these attributes of who God is.

Ask the Holy Spirit to work within you. For example, you might have a hard time embracing God as the perfect Father because you experienced a broken relationship in this area, or you may cancel God as the healer because you experienced a time when God didn't heal someone.

When we unfollow certain parts of God's character, we miss out on the fullness of who God is.

True love: Beloved, let us love one another, for love is from God, and whoever loves has been born of God and knows God. Anyone who does not love does not know God, because God is love. (1 John 4:7–8 ESV)

Father: See what great love the Father has lavished on us, that we should be called children of God! And that is what we are! The reason the world does not know us is that it did not know him. (1 John 3:1)

Powerful: O Sovereign LORD! You made the heavens and earth by Your strong hand and powerful arm. Nothing is too hard for you! (Jeremiah 32:17 NLT)

Forgiver: If we confess our sins, he is faithful and just and will forgive us our sins and purify us from all unrighteousness. (1 John 1:9)

Healer: Heal me, LORD, and I will be healed; save me and I will be saved, for you are the one I praise. (Jeremiah 17:14)

Provider: And God is able to make all grace abound to you, so that having all sufficiency in all things at all times, you may abound in every good work. (2 Corinthians 9:8 ESV)

Creator: In the beginning God created the heavens and the earth. (Genesis 1:1)

Protector: You are my hiding place; you will protect me from trouble and surround me with songs of deliverance. (Psalm 32:7)

1. Are any of these attributes hard to believe and trust?

_____

_____

_____

_____

_____

_____

_____

_____

_____

_____

_____

_____

2. Do you find yourself canceling out some of who
   God is because it makes you feel better or more
   comfortable?

_____

_____

_____

_____

_____

_____

_____

_____

_____

_____

_____

_____

3. Are there aspects of God's character you are unfollowing? If so, what could you do to embrace them?

_____

_____

_____

_____

_____

_____

_____

_____

_____

_____

_____

_____

Now that we have talked about being canceled and potentially canceling God, I want us to ask ourselves, *Are we a part of the cancel culture?* Are we the ones not showing people grace as they journey through life? Are we the ones with unforgiveness in our hearts for things people said or did years ago? Are we the ones unwilling to sit and listen to someone with a different perspective? To change a culture we must be willing to check our hearts.

1. Let's take a moment to think about the difference between unfollowing something or someone that isn't healthy for us and canceling someone. When have you unfollowed in a way that was healthy and meaningful? Have you ever canceled someone or been tempted to follow the crowd in cancel culture?

_____

_____

_____

_____

_____

_____

_____

_____

_____

_____

_____

_____

_____

_____

_____

2. Have you ever felt canceled among your friends or peers?
   What happened and how did you get through it?

_____

_____

_____

_____

_____

_____

_____

_____

_____

_____

_____

_____

_____

3. Take a personal inventory about how you interact and comment online. Do you write things you wouldn't say to someone in person? Why or why not?

_____

_____

_____

_____

who are you following? guided journal

You have a part to play in helping shift culture. Your kindness, encouragement, and grace go a long way.

The Word of God gives us the best advice and truth on how to live in the world and bring more unity, love, and peace to those around us. Let's learn from Scripture on how we can change our culture by the way we live and interact with others, both online and in real life.

meditate on the following verses:

- MATTHEW 6:14: For if you forgive other people when they sin against you, your heavenly Father will also forgive you.
- COLOSSIANS 3:13: Bear with each other and forgive one another if any of you has a grievance against someone. Forgive as the Lord forgave you.
- LUKE 6:37: Do not judge, and you will not be judged. Do not condemn, and you will not be condemned. Forgive, and you will be forgiven.
- MATTHEW 18:21–22: Then Peter came to Jesus and asked, "Lord, how many times shall I forgive my brother or sister who sins against me? Up to seven times?" Jesus answered, "I tell you, not seven times, but seventy-seven times."
- MATTHEW 6:15: But if you do not forgive others their sins, your Father will not forgive your sins.

Those verses are super convicting, especially the last one. But isn't it a better life to live knowing that you have been for-given and you don't have to hold on to the grudges or the hatred you have toward others? Let's pray that we will start to apply the truths of these scriptures and see the world become a more loving place.

prayer

God, I pray that the truth of Your Word would be applied to my life. I pray that I would not think of myself as any greater than another, and that I would be able to show grace and forgiveness to others by Your Spirit who leads me. I pray that my relationship with You would be based on truth and that it would bleed into every relationship I have.

does god
still love
me?

My mom and brother are sevens on the Enneagram.
If you know anything about the Enneagram, then
you know that sevens are the fun and free-spirited
people of the world. They love a good time and a good laugh,
and I love them for that. On the other hand, they do not like
hard conversations. Typically, when a conversation becomes difficult, they retreat. However, my mom has a different strategy

when conversations get hard—ice cream. Yup, that's right. She literally gets ice cream. One day we were having a tough conversation in the car, and the next thing I knew we were in line at Baskin-Robbins.

Before we dive into this chapter, I want to give you a warning that we are going to go deep together. But you made it all the way to chapter 8, so don't back out now! If going deep scares you and you want to put this journal down right now, I am asking you to stay with me. Give yourself some space and time as we travel through this section. I have encouraged you to be open and honest on these pages, and I am reminding you again to really let yourself "go there." Isn't that why you bought the guided journal in the first place? I encourage you to not retreat from this conversation. But if you need to, go get ice cream.

> I encourage you to not retreat from this conversation. But if you need to, go get ice cream.

Some of you might find it easy to discuss your past, your life before you came to know Jesus. For others, this might bring back memories that you'd rather not think about. Regardless of where you find yourself on this spectrum, we all have one thing in common: we were all dead in our sins and in need of Jesus to forgive us and transform our lives. And praise God that He sent His Son to do just that!

past the past

My husband is one of the most incredible people I know. He is so strong and kind, and he is absolutely in love with Jesus. When I met him, I was blown away by what a gentleman he was and how he pursued Jesus and pursued me. I didn't know any other version of him, because this was who he truly was by the time we met.

It turns out that Christian used to be a very different person. His past was not so pretty. He was wild in high school and his first semester of college, but the cool thing is that I would've never known. He ended up opening up to me and sharing with me where he was coming from, and that was one of the most vulnerable and powerful talks of our whole relationship. Not because he was hiding that side of his life but because that old self was dead. He crucified his old self with Christ and became someone new. He was no longer bound by the sin he used to walk in. Second Corinthians 5:17 says, "Therefore, if anyone is in Christ, he is a new creation. The old has passed away; behold, the new has come" (ESV).

Seeing someone convinced that they are forgiven, redeemed, and loved is a beautiful miracle and testimony. I get to see this in myself and in my husband daily. I want you to experience that same thing because the same gospel that saved us is the one offered to you.

I see the struggle that so many face when it comes to pressing past the past. The fear of who we used to be often keeps us from becoming who we are. Trust me, Christian and I both have been there. While I want to help you all get past the past, the truth is, I cannot do that. But Jesus can and already has. I want you to notice two words in the scriptures I mentioned earlier. One of those words is in 2 Corinthians 5:17, and the other one is in John 3:16. The two words are *anyone* and *whoever*. The Word of God says that if *anyone* is in Christ they are new and *whoever* believes in Him shall not perish but have eternal life! You are a part of that *anyone*—you are a part of that *whoever*.

GOD'S LOVE
IS UNENDING.

So often we exempt ourselves from the grace offered by Jesus. We think we are "too far gone." We feel we are unlovable because of what we've done. We cannot imagine how a perfect God could love someone like us. Here's the thing, friends: it's crazy, but that's what makes His love so perfect and unending. That's what makes this gospel so powerful.

Often people may try to start turning their lives around by going to church and things like that, but they still walk about feeling guilt and shame, as though God couldn't possibly love them. Friend, if you repent and give your life to Jesus, the old is gone— the new has come! Walk confidently in the forgiveness that He gave. The struggle between who we *were* and who we *are* is a tension that many of us know well. It can be difficult to let go of our past mistakes and feel confident and worthy of stepping forward in a better, more positive way—especially in the age of social media, where our pasts are never too far gone.

The fear of who we used to be often keeps us from becoming who we are.

Did you catch that? While we were *still* sinners, Christ died for us. *He knew the price He was paying when He paid it, and He did it out of love.* He showed us love right in the middle of our sin, our mess. There is no escaping our pasts, we all need God's transformation, and we all had a life before we knew His great love. I want you to know that God's love for you is established. It was proven at the cross.

No matter what your past looks like, what everyone saw you do, or maybe even what you posted on social media, you are never too far gone to become the person you know you can be in the future and the person you're called to be now. Just because you made mistakes does not mean that Jesus will love you less. In fact, those broken places are a perfect place to be met and loved by Jesus, and He can transform your whole life.

I invite you to take a moment to write down things that happened in the past that you are holding on to. Maybe it's mistakes you made and you need to repent and ask God for forgiveness. Or maybe it's mistakes others made toward you that you need to forgive them for.

Take a moment and reflect on what your journey has looked like. Use the space below to help craft your story or testimony:

STUCK IN THE PAST	FORGIVEN

1. **Life Before Christ:** *Use the space below to write out what your life was like before you came to Christ. You can use descriptive words, draw a picture, make a timeline, and so on.*

_____

_____

_____

_____

_____

_____

_____

_____

_____

_____

_____

_____

2. How You Came to Know Christ: *This is your transformation moment!*

_____

_____

_____

_____

_____

_____

_____

_____

_____

_____

_____

_____

_____

_____

3. Life After Knowing Christ:

_____

_____

_____

_____

_____

_____

_____

_____

_____

_____

_____

_____

The story of Peter hits close to home for me. He is so relatable. His intentions were always good. He was brave and a loyal friend to Jesus. Yet when times got hard, he struggled with fear, and that fear would get the best of him. That is me, too, at times.

In my relationship with Jesus I sometimes feel super confident, as though nothing could ever make me waver. And then sometimes in my journey that fear has gotten the best of me and I doubted.

Peter had moments of bravery and faith, like when he walked out on the water, and moments of fear and doubt, like when he sunk in that same water that he was so brave to walk out on seconds before. He had a moment of bravery, like the time he cut off someone's ear to stand up for Jesus, and then moments later he faced fear and doubt when he three times denied even knowing Jesus. Peter journeyed through faith just like we do. He was human and so are you. The amazing thing we need to realize is that Jesus journeyed with him.

> The amazing thing we need to realize is that Jesus journeyed with him.

Jesus was with Peter when he was brave and with him when he was fearful. He was with him when he had faith and with him when he doubted. He was there in the water when Peter began to sink, there to pick him back up and get him back to the boat. And then, after He arose from the grave, He was there to have breakfast and redeem the relationship Peter thought he had lost. Jesus is not going anywhere, friends. Your past does not scare Him. He has already paid the price for your future.

You are so much more than your past and so much more than your social media feed. We *all* need Jesus to forgive us and we *all* need Jesus to transform us. Spend time today thinking about God's massive love for you and what that means for your life and your future.

meditate on the following verses:

- ROMANS 3:23: For all have sinned and fall short of the glory of God.
- ROMANS 5:8: But God demonstrates his own love for us in this: While we were still sinners, Christ died for us.
- ROMANS 10:9–10: If you declare with your mouth, "Jesus is Lord," and believe in your heart that God raised him from the dead, you will be saved. For it is with your heart that you believe and are justified, and it is with your mouth that you profess your faith and are saved.
- MATTHEW 19:26: Jesus looked at them and said, "With man this is impossible, but with God all things are possible."

ENCOURAGEMENT

It truly is the coolest thing watching people be confident in who they are in Christ. Be confident today in your new self through Jesus!

prayer

—

Thank You for giving me the ability to press past the past. Thank You for Your grace and forgiveness for the things that I have done. I ask for strength and confidence in the new creation that I am in You.

are you following the truth or *the* truth?

When I was nineteen, I found myself in an in-between place. I had just moved to Nashville to pursue the ministry that God put on my heart. You would think that by moving I would've overcome all the fear and shame from the past and was finally going for it. You would've thought I was finally *following Jesus*. Well, sort of. I was following Jesus with my bags packed full of fear, selfishness, and shame from the past. Let's just say I was following Jesus by crawling. I wanted to run, but I wasn't quite ready to give up my baggage.

telling the truth

One day, a few months after my move, I was making small talk with a pastor when all of a sudden I felt prompted to tell her *the truth*. Not the typical, rose-colored-glasses stories and answers I told most people. The things I had been dealing with internally that no one else knew about. Next thing I knew, I could not stop sharing with her—things I had never even admitted to myself.

Have you ever had that happen? It's like your mouth is moving faster than your brain. I could not believe what I was admitting. Like why I am insecure. I told her things people spoke over me that still held me down. I told her decisions I'd made that I wasn't proud of and sins I had never repented of. I told her the whole truth. I'd never wanted to admit the truth to anyone because I felt like if I did, people would think I was a hypocrite. If I shared the truth it would be hard to relive some of the things I regret the most. And to be honest, yes, it was hard. But at the same time it was one of the most freeing things I've ever done. It was like the feeling you have when you wash your makeup off. Yes, you see your skin for what it is, but the freshness you feel is unmatched. The truth is sometimes hard to share and hard to hear. But can I tell you what is harder? Living in a lie.

After I shared everything I had walked through that got me to where I was at that moment, the pastor looked at me and said, "You need some inner healing prayer."

I was kind of embarrassed; I'm not going to lie. I was hoping she would say, "You are good to go now, thanks." As if I was just paying for a therapy session. *I finally admitted the truth. Shouldn't that have been enough?* I did not want to have to deal with any of this anymore. But I did. I finally dealt with the lies I was believing as I told the truth, and in doing so I found the truth in Jesus Christ. And that truth finally set me free.

When I look back at my story, it was in the next few months that my ministry began to take off, because I was no longer stuck in the lies. I was free.

1. Is there anything in your life you're hiding? What is it, and who would be a safe, healthy person to confess to? Can you make a plan to do this?

_____

_____

_____

_____

_____

_____

THE
TRUTH
WILL set
YOU free

2. Have you ever been in a situation where you confessed a sin you were dealing with? Was it to God or another person? What was that experience like?

_____

_____

_____

_____

_____

_____

_____

_____

_____

_____

_____

_____

3. When was the last time you let someone pray over you? What would you pray over yourself today?

_____

_____

_____

_____

_____

_____

_____

_____

_____

_____

_____

I looked up on the internet where in the Bible Jesus says, "The truth will set you free." When I did, I saw that this question was one of the top Google searches: "Where did the quote the truth will set you free come from?" I thought it was interesting that people wonder where this quote came from, knowing it's a good saying, but not fully understanding the power this quote holds because of the one who spoke the words. It comes from the Bible in John 8:31–32 (ESV): "So Jesus said to the Jews who had believed him, 'If you abide in my word, you are truly my disciples, and you will know the truth, and the truth will set you free.'"

A lot of people who claim to be Christians are not living in *the* truth—they are living *their* truth.

It's important to note that not just any truth will set you free. Only *the truth*, Jesus Christ, the truth of God's Word. A lot of people who claim to be Christians are not living in *the* truth—they are living *their* truth. And they don't understand why they're not happy, why they're not free from their sin, why they're not joyful, or why they don't have peace.

We must be confident that the Bible teaches what it teaches for a reason. Not to scare people away, but to love people in full truth. I don't want the watered-down gospel where I fill in the gaps and replace the parts that make me feel uncomfortable—I want the power of the real thing! The power that makes dead people alive again!

Take a minute in this section to be real with yourself about "truths" you have been living by that have not led you to places you want to go. Replace those with the truth of God's Word. When I think back to my life at nineteen, I was telling myself that I would just forget about the things I had done. But the truth of the Word says in James 5:16, "Therefore confess your sins to

each other and pray for each other so that you may be healed. The prayer of a righteous person is powerful and effective." Once I followed the truth and confessed my sins and allowed others to pray for me, I was healed! I no longer had to run *from* something—instead I could run *to* my purpose!

I get that it's easy to twist the truth into something we want it to be as opposed to what it actually is. Sometimes we don't even realize that's what we've done! Let's think through and identify some of these lies we're pretending are truths:

MY TRUTH	THE TRUTH
Example: I will have fun in life when I do what I want when I want.	*Example: I find full joy in doing what God wants.*

Soak in the power of these scriptures on truth.

- John 14:6 (ESV): Jesus said to him, "I am the way, and the truth, and the life. No one comes to the Father except through me."
- John 16:13 (ESV): When the Spirit of truth comes, he will guide you into all the truth, for he will not speak on his own authority, but whatever he hears he will speak, and he will declare to you the things that are to come.
- John 17:17 (ESV): Sanctify them in the truth; your word is truth.
- John 1:14: The Word became flesh and made his dwelling among us. We have seen his glory, the glory of the one and only Son, who came from the Father, full of grace and truth.
- John 18:37–38 (ESV): Then Pilate said to him, "So you are a king?" Jesus answered, "You say that I am a king. For this purpose I was born and for this purpose I have come into the world—to bear witness to the truth. Everyone who is of the truth listens to my voice." Pilate said to him, "What is truth?" After he had said this, he went back outside to the Jews and told them, "I find no guilt in him."

how to follow jesus

Following Jesus must be different from how we follow people on social media. We don't just casually click a button and watch His life from afar, swipe up on His links, get His discount code for extra blessings, and then unfollow Him when we don't find Him relevant anymore. Jesus actually addresses this idea of how to follow Him in Matthew 16:24. I'm going to put it here from the Amplified Version (AMP) so we can really understand what He was saying:

> Then Jesus said to His disciples, "If anyone wishes to follow Me [as My disciple], he must deny himself [set aside selfish interests], and take up his cross [expressing a willingness to endure whatever may come] and follow Me [believing in Me, conforming to My example in living and, if need be, suffering or perhaps dying because of faith in Me]."

You might be thinking, *Wow, following Jesus is costly.* You may just want to continue aimlessly following celebrities, trends, and methods by endless clicks and scrolls, thinking you will avoid the price. But I want you to consider: Is the cost of following worldly temptations really free? Or are you actually paying the ultimate price? Are you actually counting a greater cost by following and devoting your time to things that are essentially meaningless to saving your soul? "For what does it profit a man to gain the whole world and forfeit his soul?" (Mark 8:36 ESV).

think about this:

I have a feeling that you want more in your life then just moments of happiness, moments of fame, moments of wealth, moments of success, moments of praise, only to be met with emptiness when you lay your head down at night. A life of following Jesus may not be the easiest one, as you must learn to deny your selfish ways, but I can promise you one thing—it will be the most fulfilling.

The world can give you potentials, but the Lord can give you promises. Who are you following, friends, and where is that path leading you?

ENCOURAGEMENT

The life available to you in following Jesus will not always be easy, but it will be abundant. The power of His love and peace can satisfy the longings in your heart.

prayer
—

God, I want to follow You and You alone. I believe that Jesus is the way, the truth, and the life, the only path to get to You. I want to be led by the Spirit and not by the world. Help me to lay aside my selfish ambitions and follow You.

notes

1. Russell Heimlich, "Gen Nexters Say Getting Rich Is Their Generation's Top Goal," Pew Research Center, January 23, 2007, https://www.pewresearch.org/fact-tank/2007/01/23/gen-nexters-say-getting-rich-is-their-generations-top-goal/.
2. Christopher Osburn, "New Data Reveals Just How Desperately Millennials Want to Be Famous," Uproxx, January 25, 2017, https://uproxx.com/life/millennials-desperately-want-to-be-famous/.
3. Sharon Jayson, "Survey: Young People Who Use Social Media Seek Fame," USA Today, April 18, 2013, https://www.usatoday.com/story/news/nation/2013/04/18/social-media-tweens-fame/2091199/.
4. Benedict Carey, "The Fame Motive," New York Times, August 22, 2006, https://www.nytimes.com/2006/08/22/health/psychology/22fame.html.
5. Michael Todd (@iammiketodd), "All You Have Is All You Need. #thisisv1," video, 1:00, Facebook, September 18, 2019, https://www.facebook.com/watch/?v=767002523733295.
6. Jane Marczewski (Nightbirde), America's Got Talent, Episode 1602, aired on June 8, 2021.

acknowledgments

Thank you so much to Stephanie Vandermolen and Courtney Leatherwood. You two are incredible teammates and friends. I truly would not be able to complete this project without your help and support.

Thank you MacKenzie Howard for all of the work you poured into making this come together. You are so great to work with.

Thank you to the whole W team. Each of you makes writing a true joy. I'm grateful to work with such incredible people to make my writing better.

about the author

Sadie Robertson Huff is a *New York Times* bestselling author, speaker, influencer, and founder of Live Original. Communicating as a sister and friend, Sadie is on a mission to reach the world with the message of Christ. The host of the popular podcast *Whoa, That's Good*, which launched in 2018, she continues to top charts and minister to millions of listeners as she engages with current leaders, asking them to answer one question: "What is the best advice you have ever been given?" *Live Original*, Sadie's blog, features encouraging and transparent messages from her and her closest friends, and she is also founder of the online community and app LO Sister, which are designed to cultivate sisterhood through Bible studies and workshops. Sadie, her husband, Christian, and their daughter reside in Louisiana.

Do you want to be noticed?
Or do you want to be *known*?

In *Who Are You Following?*—and its interactive companion, *Who Are You Following? Guided Journal*, designed to enrich your study experience—Sadie shares her story of finding offline joy, guides us in taking control of social media in our lives, and helps us see what the Bible has to do with any of it. Get ready to explore how to:

- become healthier by choosing who you follow on social media
- be thoughtful about who and what you pursue online
- escape the damaging mindset of comparison and feeling *not enough*
- let go of always making yourself look like you have it all together and, instead, to rest in God's love for you
- get the *best* out of your relationship with social media and be the light in the world

Live
WHO GOD CREATED
YOU TO BE

Whether you have a long-time relationship with God or are new to faith, Sadie encourages young readers to make the most of each moment, make wise decisions, and always seek the truth of God's Word.

AVAILABLE WHERE BOOKS ARE SOLD